WISHBONES
AND
EMPTY
SPACES

PYROKARDIA

Illustrated by

Noorain Moosvi

DEDICATION

This book is dedicated to all my followers on Instagram for their love and support.

teach me how to break in beautiful

my mouth speaks in silence

my soul knows all the tales

my pen leaks out tears

CONTENTS

AUTHOR'S NOTE

Poetry is such a personal art and everyone interprets a poem differently. Titling a poem can force an interpretation in a specific path, so I'm leaving all the poems untitled with a blank space and you can fill in a title that speaks to you personally. I do hope you enjoy reading them as much I loved writing these pieces of me in words.

Every day she breaks me into pieces
maybe I'm not enough for her
maybe she needs more of me to love

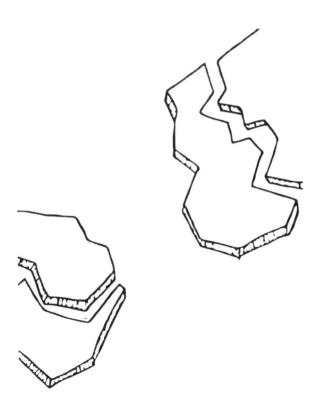

Love is the artist
we are its materials
breaking off fragments of us
trying to bring out
the masterpiece hidden within us

Tonight
hold me
remind me
what it feels like
to be unbroken

My heart fell for you
like a leaf falling in autumn
falling slowly towards the ground
swaying from side to side
loving you one minute
hating you the next
until finally it touches earth
losing every drop of reason
becoming perfectly dry
for your feet to trample on
over and over again
I guess you love the dry crunchy sound
of my leaves breaking

At night
it rains

my pillows
get soaked

and my despair
grows ever deeper

Dear Ex,
you broke all these hearts
by breaking mine

I find myself constantly on my knees, hands
clasped in supplication, begging the universe for an
answer to my question

"How can a single being occupy so much space
within me that even the whole world couldn't fill
the chasm created by her absence?"

and the answer was love
and the answer is love
and the answer will be love

If one day
you ever do look back
and you wonder
if I ever loved you
I need you to know
that I truly did
I loved you
more than life itself
I just couldn't bear
to watch you break me
over and over again

You've been hiding it for so long
but I see the truth in your eyes
I see the stars
I know you belong in the heavens
but your wings have been broken
torn off and trampled on
when I look into your eyes
I see the fears
I see the confusion
and I know you're wondering
just plain baffled
trying to figure out
what else have I come to break?

I write too much
I think too much
I love too much
I do everything too much
putting pieces of my soul
into everything I write
trying to stop writing
but I'm drowning in these thoughts
and I'm desperately
seizing every write up
like it's a bubble of oxygen
trying to stay alive
for just a minute longer
hoping that's the minute
I finally break through
to the surface
and then I'll be fine

He asked me "why are you single?"
I smiled and replied with silence
She turned to me
She didn't say a word
but I could literally hear
the wheels turning in her mind
wondering "Why are you single? When you
write so beautifully about love"
they do not realize the truth
I'm in love with love
but I'm not in love with people
I'm tired of the cycles
of loving
of breaking
of loving before picking up the pieces
so now, I'm just picking up the pieces
the shattered pieces of me
discovering what's left
figuring out what's lost
fitting what's left together
only then, can I love again

It's the empty space
inside of you
that keeps you awake
with morbid sad thoughts
and memories of better times
when the world felt alive

It's the empty space
beside you
that wakes you up at 2am
to lonely beds and cold dark nights
making you long for the days
when the world didn't feel so lonely

It's the empty spaces
that fills you up
with misery and grief
making your soul ache
the pain consuming you
until there's no space
left for life

I wonder
if the echoes
of my breaking heart
as you left me behind
in the silence
made your fading footsteps
freeze for a second
or did it hasten
your footsteps out of my life?

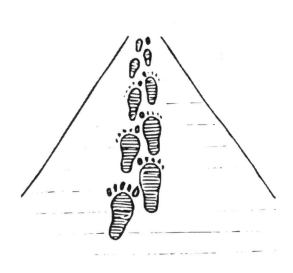

Tell me you love me
even if it's a lie

Make me smile
even if it's just for a little while

You may break my heart
but please allow me cling to my dream

Even if it's just another lie
that would last only for a little while

I'm tired of trying to fix my broken pieces into
someone else's puzzle,
hoping they'll fit
breaking myself up more trying to fit in
I've got my edges filed and rounded
I no longer recognize myself in the mirror
I'm tired and even more broken than how I started

The shattering
of my tear drops
on the ground

mimics the impact
of your exit
on my heart

You wear me down
with your toxic lies
every drop
every lie
dripping down my senses
breaking down my walls
layer beneath layer
every brick
every stone
falling for you
leaving me open
making me vulnerable
to your piercing truth

In a tiny voice, he said to her
"I'm done with love, I'll rather live forever alone
than keep getting broken"

"But, love isn't done with you, and it will never be
done, until you're made whole" his mom replied

I write these little notes
fold them into ships
hoping they sail to your port
but all they do is sink

I write these little notes
fold them into paper planes
and hope they find you
but they keep going off course

I write these little notes
in shape of hearts
wanting to give you mine
but all it ever does is break

Some days
I remember you

Some days
I remember how to smile

But never on those days
that I think of you

Words may not break your bones
but they can slip beneath your skin
and rip your soul to shreds

Break me into pieces
turn me into sludge
be the origin story
of the world's greatest art

Little by little
page by page
I write it all away
bleeding ink
breaking pens

Sometimes I wonder
if it wouldn't have been better
if I never knew love
if I never knew the euphoria of it
maybe, feeling empty
wouldn't feel so damn EMPTY

Tell me you love me
and I'll destroy the world for you

Show me you love me
and I'll break my own bones for you

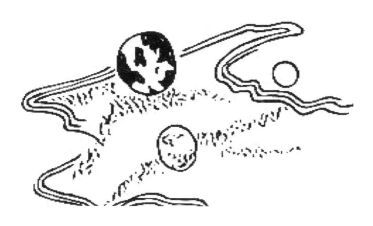

"Trust me" he said
"your heartbreak will soon be over"
I guess trust is easily promised
but it's rarely fulfilled
cause its 5 years now
and I'm still heartbroken
I trusted wrongly twice

Fall in love
break into pieces
find your true self

Beauty is a trap, I say
the roses luring
a passerby to be torn

Beauty is a trap, I say
the candle flame enticing
a moth to burn

Beauty is a trap, I say
as I lie bleeding
slowly turning stiff

Beauty is a trap, I say
as I lie here breaking
at the bottom of her cliff

Sometimes the words "I'm tired"
are not break up lines

I'm simply just tired of loving you
but never getting loved in return

Tired of waiting
holding on, hoping you'll change

Sometimes the words "it's over"
is said in the hopes
that you won't actually let it be over

Break my heart quietly
with my back turned
so I don't have to know you've left

Let me live on
clinging to the illusions
of the memories we shared

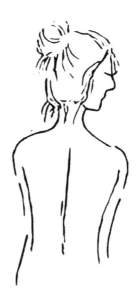

We fell
into the book of love
stumbling through the pages
filling up the paragraphs
creating new chapters
right till the very last page
where we fell
out of the book
breaking into pieces
as we fell apart

They will break you
as if breaking you
is the only process
through which they can
ever feel whole again

The problem isn't that you broke my heart
my problem is that you didn't break my heart at a
single instant
so that I could heal from that moment on
you broke my heart at several instances
every time I think of you
every time I hear our song on the radio
every time I hear your name randomly called by a
stranger
every time I see a stranger carrying your shoulders
or flipping your hair
every time I see a memory of you through the
corners of my eyes
you break me at several points in time
setting me back every time I thought I've healed
from you
your memories break me everyday
can you please come back?
break me all at once
and never leave again?

Whenever you need me
you'll find me
in pieces
in love
still waiting
for you
to fill up my spaces

Maybe someday
I'll be able to look at you
and feel absolutely nothing

Maybe someday
you'll look at me
and you'll feel everything

Maybe someday
someone's heart will break
and for once, it wouldn't be mine

Every time I break
my bones get stronger
weighing me down
every time I try to fly
off love's precipice

Every time I break
I like to think
my bones
are being hollowed out
making me lighter
and I hope that
the next time
I fall off love's ledge
I'll achieve flight

They say
a picture is worth
a thousand words
maybe, that's why
seeing your picture
breaks my heart
into a million pieces

———————————

And eventually
you found out
how good it feels
to feel nothing but emptiness
deeper than the eyes
and you've felt safer
with everyone that tried
to love you after that
knowing that when they leave
you'll feel no pain
but you'll always wonder if
they would have stayed
if you could have chanced
just a little more danger

It always amazes me
how light these tears are
cupped in the palm
of your hands
when they felt heavy enough
to break my heart

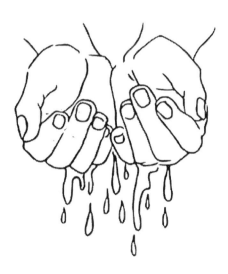

I fall in love with people I find portions of you in
that's why I could only love them but a fraction of
what I felt for you

I guess we are all meant to be broken
losing bits and pieces of our hearts
trying to fit in another broken heart
until we find the right kind of broken
to make us whole again

I'm a broken vessel
love me at your peril
pour your love into me
and you would never fill me up

I'm broken into pieces
clutch me to your heart
and I'll slip through your fingers
tearing you into pieces too

Your love is a wild fire,
burning me up

Consuming every piece of me
until I was but a black hole
unable to be filled.

Forever empty and hungry for love,
sucking it all in
yet incapable of ever being filled

Hell
is an empty space
where your memories live

Hell
is the place
where I choose to live

Ever smiled when you're listening to a very sad
song?
not because you're happy
but cause in that piece of music
you kind of feel complete and you know there's
someone out there that understands exactly how
you're feeling
that's how you make me feel
broken, but in good company

I've got pieces of me
embedded in tracks of music
and every replay
is a reminder
of all the memories
I've kept buried
deep within my mind
dredging them up to the surface
until, I've got a video
running inside my head
to the sound of the music

I've given pieces of myself away
into people's souls
in different nations
on several continents
losing myself
in heady moments of emotions
that ends all too quickly
losing fragments of me
until I've not got enough
of me left

I loved you
despite your past
I never cared about the stories
I only loved you
but that wasn't enough

Even as we fell apart
me, grabbing at every falling piece
trying not to lose even a tiny bit of you
you slithered through
the spaces between my fingers

Now, I'm all alone
with fists clenched around half-formed dreams
ghostly echoing whispers of your voice
telling me you'll stay forever
haunting me in my soul's cavern

Let your love slip into the spaces
between the broken pieces of my heart
let it fill me up
let it seal up my gaps
let it make me whole

Treat her soul like an archaeological dig
for ancient treasure. Dig patiently along
the edges of her, loving every single
piece you unearth. Don't go too fast, for
the tunnel you're digging may just collapse on
you.

Life has taught me to hide pieces of myself away
making me feel incomplete
sometimes those hidden pieces are lost to me
and I'm stuck trying to find myself in a world
trying to tear more pieces out of me
some days, I'm more of myself than I've ever been
some days, I feel less than I know I should be

Look to the dark night sky
and see the pieces of my broken heart
all dead but still shining
hoping to catch your eyes once again

She's got a little piece of the moon within her heart
reflecting every little bit of the goodness around
her into the world
lighting up the shadows within the hearts of the
world

I keep sharing my heart
splitting it down the middle
for the ones I love
living on half of a heart
then down to a quarter
when the love went numb
and I had to love another
so promise me you'll stay
before I have to learn to breathe
on one-eighth of a heart
cause I know deep in my bones
there's no living
on just one-sixteenth of a heart

Here I go again
writing about the ones that broke me
always playing the good guy
while standing over the bones of the ones
I've got buried in my crypt
piles of broken bones
bones white
bones shattered
bones pounded into dust
bones with meat still stuck on them
that I return to gnaw at sometimes
hairs sticking into my teeth after I'm done
leaving behind just enough meat
for another visit
so this is to the girls
the ones I've hurt
and the ones I'm hurting
I'm not a good guy
that I know very well
I'm just trying to do the best I can
and sometimes that is enough
but most times its not

I really wish
I could be that person
that wishes you the best
that wishes you find the right one
as I lay here
with a broken wish bone
wrapped around my heart
but I'm not

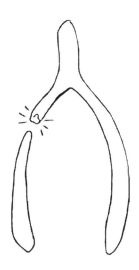

And I hope
by the time these bones start aching
your smile will still be my soothing balm

With every poem
I write
my heart breaks
just a little more
the emotions seeping out
through the cracks
onto these pages
little by little
until it becomes an
uncontrollable flood
leaving me drained
empty and weak
in your eyes

Some people come into your life
create a niche for themselves
in a corner of your soul
and stay there
until they gradually become an integral part of you
becoming the centerpiece
then they leave
cutting out everything that is them
away from you
and you can feel that space
within you
like an empty chasm
a void within you
it's empty
but it weighs full

I'm done waiting
for my empty spaces
to be filled by
someone else

I'm going to
grow into them
by myself

She asked me "what are you afraid of?"
I replied "I'm afraid of nothing"

She said "even losing me?"
I told her again "I'm afraid of nothing"

She fumed and stormed off
leaving "nothing" behind

in the silence
devoid of her voice

in the darkness
devoid of her color

I poured everything I've got into you
and I got nothing back
until I was empty and drained
of all feelings for you
cause you didn't refill me
cause you gave nothing back
now, there's nothing left to give
so I'll take my leave

Nothing scares me
nothing excites me
as much as loving you

I look out my window
I see the sun shining
the clouds floating lazily in the blue sky
the birds are singing happily
people walking around
with smiles on their stupid faces
without a care
as they hurry to their various destinations
no one knows
nothing knows
that I'm dead inside
and I wonder how can life go on
how does the living keep on living?
why isn't your absence
causing a disruption in the natural order?
how did life keep the same?
how will I keep the same
now that you're gone?

It takes a whole lot to love me
to love my broken heart
it takes a brave person
to hug my heart with theirs
despite the sharp edges
piercing through them
bleeding them out
till there's nothing left

I'm scared of the dark
and every silence
makes me shiver
so I overcompensate
filling in the nothingness
with everything
and that's even scarier
for within this everything
lies a greater madness
a loneliness of self
suspended between everything
that never mattered

All she's got left
are the broken
burnt out sticks
of the loves
she had once lighted
so forgive her
if she's reluctant
to light another flame
for your temporary love

Find someone
who sees
your broken pieces
as a puzzle
to be put back whole

Do not fall
for someone
who is not ready
to pick up
your broken pieces

You're not in love
if everything she does
doesn't break you

There's no feeling of completeness
to be attained with someone
who keeps tearing you down

Whenever people
throw their hearts
at me
like throwing stars
it cuts me up
and I bleed
I stand in the light
and smile at them
with eyes
full of love

Whenever I throw
my heart out
at people
like shurikens
they weave
and my love
gets lost into
space
I crawl into
darkened corners
with eyes
full of rejected tears
and still love them
anyway

I wish to thank everyone
that ever broke me

for giving me the opportunity

to see into my core
it's beautiful in there

to rearrange my pieces
into a stronger form

The heart weighs
more heavily
when it's in pieces

I wonder how I'm suppose
to give you my all
when all I feel inside is emptiness

It is the silence between us
that scares me

It is the blank canvas
I paint my worries on

It is the blank page
I write my fears in

Pictures of us walking away
Tales of our ending

Like the tide
I come in for sometime
then I leave

I mean no harm
my heart is just too broken
to ever hold its shape

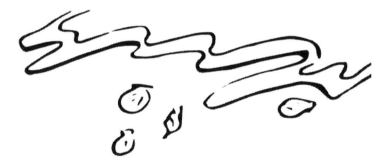

Maybe I'm using up too much of the love
we should share

Maybe I need to love you
a little less

Then maybe you'll love me
a little more

You've ruined me for love
we can't be together
I can't unlove you
there's no other you

Your love
left a mark
in my heart

A fingerprint
of your soul

Which
nobody else
can unlock

I said to her "Dear, I can't love you. I've been
hollowed out, emptied and drained, an empty well
only meant to be filled with stones"

She held my hands, looked into my eyes and said
to me, "My dear, people like you are never empty,
your well may be dry right now, but when the
raining season comes, your well will be full once
again. And I'll be there, when that happens"

and my eyes overflowed

His heart is filled with the flames of his emotions
every single breath seeming to fuel the flames
even more
burning ever brighter
until there was nothing left but a husk

Let me write on the scars of your heart
every line telling of how much I love you
until the scars don't show anymore
and all you see is my love for you

I still wake up everyday
hoping that maybe today
you'll wake up
and come back to me

I miss you
though you are right next to me

I miss you
cause you aren't the you anymore

I'm stuck
with the regret

of not finding you
of not loving you

in all the times
I was lost

in all the times
I was empty

I've healed wrong
maybe I need to be broken again
maybe then, I'll heal right

The slow drip of my tears
tells a two-faced lie
of the storm raging inside of me

The empty silence
after every "I love you"
slowly and quietly
raising the tombstone
of our love over
my too loud beating heart

I miss the days
when all I've got
within my heart
was oxygen
and it didn't hurt
just to breathe

When you left
you took all the stars
away with you
leaving me all alone
in the dark night sky
blood red moon
unwanted by anyone

The tear drops
rolling down my cheeks
aren't cause you left me
not caused by an heartbreak
my eyes tear up
from the smoke
coming from my dreams of us
sitting on a porch
watching the sunset
as our grandkids play in the yard
getting burnt to ashes
filling the air
choking me up
making it hard
oh, so very hard
for me to breathe

It's a never ending cycle
of broken hearts

Our tears
cascading down like dominoes

You break me
cause you were broken by another

There's no one to blame
yet we're all at fault

Too many times
I wake up
just wishing
I could still wish
it was over

I kept on waiting
for hours
for days

Waiting for an answer
for a single whisper
for a single gesture

So I took the silence
and the lack of action
for an answer

and I filled the silence
with my fading footsteps

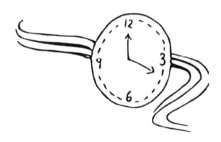

Stop trying so hard
You don't need to try so hard for someone
who loves you
Don't keep on trying harder and harder
Until you break yourself
And someone who don't want you whole
Wouldn't want you when you're in pieces

I called on you
to sit with me
by the stream
of my tears
to watch with me
the broken halo
of the sunset
over our love
but as always
you're never there
every single time
my world goes dark

I hate you
I swear, I wish it's true
I wish I could hate you
hate your smiles
and how you made me feel
I hate all the memories we shared
I wish I could erase them
like they never happened
I hate you
please come back

I'm tired of feeling
like a repairman

There to heal
your broken pieces

Then you leave
until you get broken again

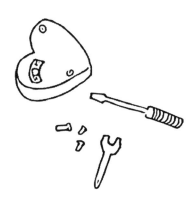

Loneliness became me
when I found you
yet, you weren't mine

Listen to me
to the silence
between my heart beats
my heart don't skip
for you anymore

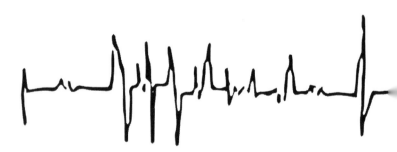

It's hard to fall in love now
not cause I don't want to
cause I crave it so much

It's really hard to love
when every time I try
it feels like I'm settling

It's hard, very very hard
when you've fallen in love once
and it felt so perfect

I guess it's hard to love
when you're still in love
with the one that broke you

Every time I fall
for someone new
don't tell me it's beautiful

Every time I fall
just like a leaf
I fear it's the end of me

She loves me
She loves me not
I'm tearing out this flower's petals
while you're tearing my heart out

My body walked away
leaving my heart behind

my body
knows better than to stay

but my heart
still thinks you're home

She's got
broken full moons
in her eyes
from all the werewolves
that spend the nights
howling at her
only to disappear
into human bodies
every time the sun comes up
each morning

One day, I'll find that person that's going to make me feel more than okay. Someone whose mere entry into my life would be a cause for celebration. Someone to share my sadness with. Someone I can call at anytime of the day and wouldn't be too busy. Someone who would make me feel wanted, needed and adored. Someone I don't need to hide my pains from. Someone I can be real with, that will break me and stay to mend my pieces back whole. Someone who will stay, someone I'll end with.

I'm afraid to sleep now
though my dreams are beautiful
they are always about you
but when I wake up
you are no longer here with me
and my heart breaks afresh
I lose you all over again everyday

They tell me
time heals all wounds
but all I feel is numb
as I bleed everything away
until I feel nothing at all
at least, for most of the time
but sometimes, when I'm all alone
or even in the midst of a crowd
I choke up with everything
I've been holding back
and in those moments
I learn the hard truth
time is but a bandage
and sometimes, the emotions bleed through

Maybe we need
to be broken,
for the light within
to beam across
the shoreline
deep into the seas
to guide the soul mate
safely through the
treacherous rocks
into our arms

So many times
I thought I've lost it all
thinking there's nothing else
nothing else left to lose
but the world
keeps taking away from the nothing
disabusing me of the illusion
that I've got nothing
telling me
I've got everything within the nothing
if I will only open up my eyes to see

Let's make a toast
   to all the ones
   who loved us
   then broke us

   to all the fuck yous
   we never said
   cause we still hoped

   to all the loves
   and the fuck yous
   that died unfulfilled

.

It's the waiting
that keeps us wanting

It's the waiting
that keeps us hoping

It's the waiting
that keeps us breaking

I sit out
under the moonlight dark
always wondering

how do you not break?
how do you not bleed?

fold up into an origami
tucking in everything
you ever held dear
away from the world

curl up into a ball
hoping to roll away
from all the pains

can someone please tell me
how do I ever stop breaking
how can I stop bleeding?

Don't ask me
if I've ever been broken
cause I've never known broken
all I've known is burning
every breathe suffocating
every vein burning
as the pain chase down
the oxygen in my veins
the flames racing
through my blood
so please
do not ask me if I'm broken
when all that's left of me
is ashes

ABOUT THE AUTHOR

Pyrokardia is the pen name for Ogunfowodu Olufemi. He is the author of *A Beautiful Mess*.

He is a physiotherapist. An indigene of Ijebu-Ode, Ogun state, Nigeria. Hobbies includes searching for relatively unknown rock bands to love, reading fantasy novels, playing fantasy games and considers himself a citizen of too many worlds. Favourite game for now is Elder Scrolls (Skyrim).

You can read more of his works on Instagram (@pyrokardia)

42413870R00078

Made in the USA
Middletown, DE
10 April 2017